The Crock-Pot Cookbook:

2000 Days of Delicious and Creative Recipes for Every Slow Cooking Meal | Transform Your Dishes with Economical Slow-Cooking Techniques

By:
Reese Irwin

© **Copyright 2024 - All rights reserved.**

This book's contents cannot be copied, duplicated, or transmitted without the publisher's or author's express written consent.

The publisher and author disclaim all liability for any losses, claims, or financial damages resulting from the material in this book. Not in a direct or indirect way.

Legal Notice:

Copyright protects this book. This book is solely meant for individual use. No part of this work may be reproduced, distributed, sold, quoted, or paraphrased without the publisher's or author's consent.

Disclaimer Notice:

Please be aware that the information in this publication is solely meant to be used for amusement and education. We've done everything we can to provide accurate, up-to-date, trustworthy, and comprehensive information. There are no expressed or implied guarantees of any kind. The reader understands that the writer is not providing professional, financial, medical, or legal advice. This book's content was compiled from a number of sources. Please do not undertake any of the practices in this book without first consulting a licensed specialist.

By using the information in this document, the reader acknowledges and agrees that the author shall not be held responsible for any direct or indirect loss resulting from the use of such material, including but not limited to errors, omissions, or inaccuracies.

Table of Contents

Introduction 5

Chapter 1: The Crock Pot Chronicles 8

Chapter 2: How to Choose a Slow Cooker 15

Chapter 3: Decoding the Science of Slow Cooking 19

Chapter 4: Slow Cooker Vs. Crock-Pot 23

Chapter 5: The Benefits of Slow Cooking 28

Chapter 6: FAQs 35

Chapter 7: Breakfast Recipes 38

1. Apple Crumble Breakfast Pudding 38
2. Honey Sweet Raisin Bread 39
3. Silky Smooth Hot Chocolate 41
4. Sweet Morning Chocolate Rice Pudding 42
5. Baked Beans with Wedges 42
6. Honey Granola and Blueberry Yogurt 44
7. Fruity and Spiced Butter Spread 45
8. Slow Cooked Cinnamon Applesauce 46
9. Easy Bacon and Egg Casserole 47
10. Maple and Blueberry Steel Cut Oatmeal 48
11. Cinnamon-Raisin French Toast Breakfast 49
12. Lavender Infused Blueberry Jam 50
13. Crockpot Oatmeal 51
14. Vegan Pumpkin Spice Syrup 52

15.	Strawberry French Toast	53
16.	Sweet Cinnamon Swirled Pancake	54
17.	Vegan Omelet	55
18.	Healthy Oats and Quinoa Breakfast	56
19.	Oats with Quinoa	57
20.	Classic Strawberry Rhubarb Jam	58

Chapter 8: Lunch Recipes 59

21.	Mustard-Crusted Salmon	59
22.	Thai Clear Chicken Soup	60
23.	Easy CrockPot Meatballs	61
24.	Turkey Soup with Rosemary and Kale	62
25.	Mustard Garlic Shrimps	63
26.	Spicy Basil Shrimp	64
27.	Express Shrimps and Sausage Jambalaya Stew	64
28.	Crockpot Chicken Curry	65
29.	Five-Spice Tilapia	66
30.	Lemon Parsley Chicken	67
31.	Basic Shredded Chicken	67
32.	CrockPot Fajita Chicken	68
33.	Onion and Bison Soup	69
34.	CrockPot Yellow Chicken Curry	70
35.	Fiesta Pork Chops	71
36.	Chipotle Chicken Enchilada Stew	72
37.	Lamb's Feet Soup	73
38.	Herb-Crusted Pork Chops	74
39.	Herbed Pork Tenderloin	74
40.	Prosciutto-Wrapped Scallops	75

Chapter 9: Dinner Recipes 77

41.	Cheesy Ranch Chicken	77
42.	Classic Pork Adobo	78
43.	CrockPot Beef Picadillo	79

44.	Spicy Pork with Mapo Tofu	80
45.	Coconut Turmeric Chicken	81
46.	CrockPot Beef Rendang	81
47.	Citrus infused Chicken Breasts	82
48.	Homey Tomato Soup	83
49.	Butternut Squash Soup	84
50.	Spicy Indian Beef Roast	85
51.	Popeye's Turkey Soup	86
52.	Italian Meatball Soup	87
53.	CrockPot Gingered Pork Stew	88
54.	Three-Bean Vegan Chili	89
55.	Beef Tomato Lentil Soup	90
56.	Silky Broccoli and Cheese Soup	91
57.	Split Pea Soup	92
58.	Chipotle Chicken Soup	93
59.	French Canadian Pea Soup	94
60.	Cajun Sausage and White Bean Soup	95

Chapter 10: Dessert Recipes 97

61.	Mandarin Cream	97
62.	Mascarpone With Strawberry Jelly	98
63.	Easy Monkey Rolls	99
64.	Lemony Orange Marmalade	100
65.	Braised Pears	100
66.	Stuffed Peaches	101
67.	Cinnamon Rice Milk Cocktail	102
68.	Mango Cream Dessert	102
69.	Apricot Spoon Cake	103
70.	Baked Goat Cheese Balls	104

Conclusion 105

Introduction

Picture arriving home on a cold winter's evening to the comforting smell of a filling stew simmering on the stove. After a long day of laboring outside, you are welcomed home by the comforting warmth of the heaters and the delicious aroma of a dinner that has been patiently cooking in your dependable crock pot. Instead of spending the better part of the day laboring in the kitchen, you just mixed the ingredients, put them in the oven, and watched the magic happen.

But for a lot of people, a crock pot is more of an outdated, misunderstood artifact hidden in the back of the cabinet, a reminder of unfulfilled culinary potential than a necessity. Put otherwise, the crock pot represents wasted culinary potential. Why? For some people, finding recipes that are easy to make and delicious could be challenging. Some people avoid eating anything that is made in a crock pot because they have been misled into thinking that the flavors are the same. Many people in today's fast-paced culture have forgotten how to use a slow cooker, even though there are numerous advantages to utilizing one.

You will fall in love with this humble piece of equipment all over again after this gastronomic revelation.

Why should you read all of this garbage and waste your time? Above all, you are going to be inundated with recipes that will persuade you that slow cooking is the way to go. Imagine a menu that would make even the most varied restaurant blush, with flavors that singe your senses and textures that flow with you. You can expect each dish to yield the maximum flavor with the least amount of effort.

Additionally, you will discover how to customize your crock pot to cook foods from other cuisines, making each meal a special and delightful experience rather than a chance discovery. You'll be astonished at the variety of dishes you can make in your slow cooker, ranging from a delectable chocolate lava cake to a chicken dish with a Mediterranean taste profile.

But the food isn't the only highlight of the occasion. The main concept of this collection is regaining control over your schedule. We know it's not always practical to spend a lot of time in the kitchen because there are so many other demands on your time. You'll be able to accomplish more in the allocated time because these meals don't require continuous attention. It is feasible for you to make a delicious meal while working and a delicious breakfast while you are asleep.

"Who is the great mind behind this wisdom taught by the crock pot?" is perhaps what you're wondering. Not only is the chef behind these recipes very skilled, but they are also big fans of slow cooking. Each dish in this book has been created with a great deal of care and attention to detail, ensuring that it is delicious and easy to make. Their knowledge is the result of a lifelong passion for flavorful cuisine, an appreciation for the time-saving benefits of the crock pot, and a dedication to honing their culinary skills over the course of a lifetime.

Once you've read this book, you'll realize that the crock pot is more than simply a useful kitchen tool. It will prove to be a reliable partner in the kitchen, helping you to quickly prepare delicious meals. Your crock pot will be waiting for you with the promise of a wonderful and simple dinner when life gets too hard to handle and you just can't stand going into the kitchen.

This book is a blessing for anyone who has ever laughed at the thought of cooking, for anyone who has ever wished that home-cooked meals didn't require as much work to prepare, and for anyone who wants to discover the culinary miracles that slow cooking can provide. Accept it and set off on a delicious adventure that will leave you with more free time and a greater sense of fulfillment from your palate.

Here we are at the start of what will soon be the second golden age of the crock pot. I hope your dinner was utterly delicious!

Chapter 1:
The Crock Pot Chronicles

What is a Crock Pot?

You're relaxing in your cozy kitchen when all of a sudden you're transported back in time to a time-honored recipe that your grandmother used to swear by: slow-cooked beef stew. You consider going for the dependable kitchen appliance known as the Crock Pot, which is renowned for bringing such dishes to life, while the idea tantalizes your taste buds.

You'll notice that there's a common misconception about the Crock Pot below. The phrase is frequently used in casual conversation and is synonymous with "slow cooker," independent of the appliance's maker or brand. In technical terms, "Crock Pot" refers to a brand that has come to be associated with the device itself, just like "Kleenex" is often used for tissues of any kind or "Xerox" for photocopying. Put differently, "slow cooker" is now commonly referred to as "Crock Pot." A slow cooker, as the name implies, allows food to be cooked over an extended length of time. This makes it the quintessential "one-pot" gadget, perfect for cooking foods that bring out the greatest tastes after a little time for the flavors to meld. Among its most well-known products? stews and soups that will cheer you up, as well as softly prepared meats. What's the secret? because it ensures that every element of the finished meal contributes to its overall coherence through the careful and level distribution of heat it offers.

How to use the Crock Pot

One who has a Crock Pot is like someone who owns a cauldron of mystical ingredients. It is simple, effective, and nearly hard to do incorrectly. Nevertheless, there is a method to learning it, just like with any other kind of magic.

Temperature: The Crock Pot typically has two distinct operating modes: LOW and HIGH. Think of each of these as a stand-alone chapter within the greater story. Your food will cook in a shorter amount of time—possibly as little as four hours—if you choose the HIGH option, which moves through the storyline swiftly. Conversely, the LOW option doubles that time to almost eight hours as it meanders and takes its time. The course of the story will vary slightly depending on the choice you select. It is advisable to refer to the user manual of your device and follow the timing guidelines provided in the recipe you select.

Size and servings: Let's say you're hosting a large party and there won't be enough food for everyone to eat from the main course you've been preserving in your slow cooker. Select a Crock Pot size that corresponds with your typical serving needs to prevent such a disaster. Remember that overindulging in fillings is a social faux pas. A dish that is overflowing with ingredients may not cook evenly, resulting in a dish that is more like a culinary cacophony than a delectable symphony. To ensure delicious results, always maintain the level at no more than two-thirds capacity.

Time: Life is full with activities. Occasionally, the stress of the day prevents you from having time to watch what you eat. With your Crock Pot, there's no need for it. Turn the heat down to LOW, leave your dish to cook slowly for about 8 hours, and when you come back, it will have transformed into a delicious meal. Furthermore, should you be running late, your device, playing the part of a loyal butler, will keep the meal WARM, guaranteeing that it stays at the perfect temperature until you're ready to eat it.

Liquids: Using a slow cooker, like a Crock Pot, modifies standard cooking methods in certain ways. For instance, liquids evaporate faster in regular pots and pans, resulting in concentrated taste residue. However, when it comes to the crock pot, things aren't quite the same. Liquids remain consistent in their consistency. As such, proceed with caution while incorporating them. Which would you like to use in your dish—cream or wine? You might want to start by using the cooktop to chop them down. If you are using a slow cooker, though, you should trust the directions that the recipe provides.

Embracing slow cooking can provide a certain quiet beauty in this fast-paced environment. It seems almost defiant. Amidst the craze for instant gratification, one kitchen appliance—the crock pot, in particular—has come to represent tolerance, affection, and the luxury of time. These diaries explore a culinary culture that has inspired many home cooks and professional chefs to slow down, appreciate the craft of cooking, and take a step back from kitchen gadgets.

The general word for slow cookers, which includes the well-known Crock-Pot brand, is "slow cookers." These appliances are now commonplace in the kitchens of many homes worldwide. The popularity of slow cooking has made it feasible to cook food slowly, producing delectable and tender dishes with little effort. The following provides a quick overview of the Crock-development Pot's and history:

1. Origins: Cooking food for a prolonged amount of time over low heat has been done for ages. Food was sometimes cooked in traditional societies by submerging ceramic pots in furnaces or hot coals and heating the contents over several hours. Conversely, the 20th century is where the slow cooker that we use today first appeared.
2. The "Cattle": Irving Naxon named his created frying apparatus the "Naxon Beanery," and he received a patent for it in 1940. Naxon's creative inspiration came from stories his grandmother told him about cooking cholent, a traditional Jewish stew, in her town bakery oven in Lithuania. The Beanery was a simple device that had three parts: a heating element, a removable pot, and an outer shell. It was essentially responsible for the invention of the modern slow cooker.
3. Rival Purchases Naxon: The Beanery's plans were acquired when the Rival Company bought Naxon Utilities Corporation at the start of the 1970s. The appliance was rebranded by Rival as the "Crock-Pot" and sold to American homes under that name.
4. The 1970s Boom Throughout the 1970s, the Crock-Pot brand significantly increased its market share, especially in the US. The increasing number of women entering the workforce at the time made the convenience of slow cookers more and more evident. Dinner could be made in the morning, left to simmer all day, and then served to the family in the evening when they got home.
5. Enhancements & Features: Over the years, the Crock-Pot has experienced a number of redesigns that have affected both its look and functionality. Many different heat settings, programmable digital

timers, and even "keep warm" features—which guarantee that food is kept at the proper temperature without overcooking—are common features of the more modern versions. Furthermore, innovations like locking lids, which facilitate transportation, and stovetop-safe inserts that brown safely have expanded the range of applications.
6. Differentiations & Rivalsry: As Crock's popularity grew, so did the demand for comparable household appliances. Pot's Over time, the term "slow cooker" became more widely used, and other manufacturers entered the market with unique perspectives on the device. Not only can slow cookers do the usual things, but some of them can also brown, sauté, or steam food.
7. Current Trends: A lot of cooking shows, internet food blogs, and digital pinboards like Pinterest have contributed to the recent surge in popularity of slow-cooked foods. This, along with the growing popularity of home-cooked meals and meal preparation, has solidified the place of Crock-Pots in modern kitchens.

Social And Cultural Influences On Slow Cooking.

1. Traditional Lifestyles: Before the development of contemporary conveniences, a wide range of societies lived according to methods of subsistence like farming or hunting, which necessitated spending a large amount of the day outside of their homes. Slow cooking allowed for the preparation of dinner in the morning, which could then be left to cook all day, ensuring a warm meal when the cook came back in the evening.
2. Economic Aspects Slow cooking is a way to cut food costs. Occasionally more chewy, less expensive cuts of meat become soft and delicious when cooked gently. For this reason, it is a desirable option for families or communities looking to maximize their resources.

3. Location & Climate: Slow-cooked stews and soups provide warmth and nourishment in various situations, especially those that are cooler. Cooking at a slow temperature can also provide heat for a residential building. Additionally, slow cooking might be more affordable in some areas if wood or coal is used as the primary fuel source.
4. Festivities & Rituals of Different Cultures: During rituals or celebrations, traditional delicacies from numerous cultures are made slowly. For example, consider the North African tagine, the Jewish Shabbat cholent, or the Hawaiian luau pig. These foods often represent more than just a meal but rather an occasion shared with a group of people and are deeply embedded in the cultural fabric.
5. Safety: Gradual cooking at a low temperature was a technique used before refrigeration to guarantee that food was cooked through and lower the risk of foodborne illness. This was particularly true for dishes that featured a variety of components or that utilized every part of an animal.
6. Taste & Texture: Slow cooking produces a unique flavor and texture that are highly valued in many different cultural contexts. Flavors can be blended gradually over an hour to create a depth and complexity that is hard to achieve with faster cooking methods.
7. Modern-Day Convenience: With the advent of the modern slow cooker, like the Crock-Pot, it is now possible to prepare a home-cooked meal at the end of the day without needing someone to be present to oversee the cooking process. As society grew busier and more families had two working parents, this was especially beneficial.
8. Health & Wholesomeness: Using natural cooking techniques and whole ingredients in food preparation has become more popular in recent years. Because slow cooking doesn't require the use of fats or

oils like frying or sautéing does, some people think it's a healthier cooking technique. Furthermore, it often yields an entire dinner—grains, vegetables, and proteins—that can be made in a single pot.
9. Community & Sharing: Slow-cooked meals are typically served in a community environment due to the quantity of food prepared and the complexity of the dishes. A few instances of how they promote a sense of community and sharing are potluck meals, neighborhood feasts, and family get-togethers.
10. Fusion Cooking and Globalization: As a result of growing global connectivity, many cooking techniques have come together. It is possible for two cultures to borrow and modify each other's slow cooking methods to produce new and intriguing dishes.

Chapter 2:
How to Choose a Slow Cooker

The world of slow cookers is vast, intricate, and full of delectable food options. A slow cooker that fits your needs can be a trustworthy companion, regardless of your level of experience in the kitchen. Let's examine the specifics of the matter and see what considerations should be made while choosing the best slow cooker for your home kitchen.

1. Size of the Slow Cooker

There is a whole rainbow of sizes available, from the small portable 1-quart model to the massive 22-quart roaster. The most compact model is transportable. Size matters for preserving the dish's overall quality as a culinary production as well as for figuring out the right serving size. You incur the risk of overcooking the meal if you overfill the pan, but you also run the risk of undercooking it if you underfill it.

This is how a more straightforward equation might appear: For every pound of beef, you need one quart of space. Because of this, a five-pound roast requires a five-quart pot. Regarding portions:

- For a romantic meal for two, a serving size of one to three quarts is suitable.
- A 4 to 5 pint capacity could be sufficient for a couple or small family.
- Larger families or those who like to host parties can benefit from 6- or 7-quart containers.

Placement is an additional consideration. If you store your slow cooker in an easily accessible place, it will get more use. Additionally, there are cookers with interchangeable inserts that function similarly to many cookers without the mess that comes with them.

2. Shape and Style of the Slow Cooker

When choosing a slow cooker, there are several forms to take into account in addition to the conventional spherical slow cookers that work well for stews and soups. Larger portions of meat and meat with bones can be served best in the oval and rectangular shapes. Furthermore, they may be effortlessly incorporated into various kitchen designs, optimizing the utilization of your countertop area.

Both black and stainless steel have surfaces that are simple to keep clean, which adds to their modern appeal. However, those with a taste for the theatrical can choose from a wide range of hues and patterns. Do you intend to travel with your culinary creation? The best way to stop spillage is to use a lid with a locking mechanism.

3. Construction of the Slow Cooker

Having settings that heat up and cool down fast is beneficial in preventing the creation of bacteria. A slow cooker's design, especially if it's smooth and uncrackable, ensures that the appliance is easy to clean and helps inhibit the formation of bacteria. Stainless steel gives a more refined touch, but it takes a little more maintenance to preserve its brilliance than other metals.

4. Slow Cooker Inserts

All the action and excitement happens in the insert, which is housed inside the cooker. Stoneware or ceramic crocks hold heat better than other types, resulting in more consistent cooking. They are resilient and easy to clean up after usage. Usually featured in cookers that are good for sautéing, metal inserts offer versatility. Some can be prepared on the stovetop and then frozen, microwaved, or popped into the oven. You should look for inserts with ergonomic handles and detachable designs because security and portability are critical factors.

5. Temperature Controls and Features

The debate over digital versus manual approaches is still very much alive. Using a manual slow cooker requires you to be present at the end of the cooking period due to the simple knob controls. They won't be extremely expensive, but they will require your time. On the other hand, those that are programmable feature timers that can be pre-programmed and that can automatically transition to keep-warm modes. Even voice assistants like Alexa work with the most latest versions. Purchasing a multi-cooker that can cook rice in addition to its other applications can be a wise investment if you like the idea of having several uses.

6. Slow Cooker Control Panel

The two most crucial factors are accessibility and visibility. A well-lit, intuitive control panel not only makes cooking more enjoyable, but it also highlights the value of safety and is simpler to clean.

7. Slow Cooker Lids

It is imperative that clarity and comfort be provided. Glass or plastic covers that are clear allow light to pass through without losing heat. A loose lid that lets steam escape and splatters can be a recipe for catastrophe in the kitchen.

8. Slow Cooker Accessories

The appropriate accessories can make a big impact when slow cooking. By using safe utensils and protecting your surfaces with a cutting board below, you can help prevent damage to the insert. Slow cooker liners may turn into your greatest ally very quickly if cleaning isn't your favorite pastime. And if you're really adventurous, you may use the double-lining technique to produce two different dishes at once.

9. Slow Cooker Spare Parts

It is wise to find out if the model you have chosen has replacement components available for purchase. You may find out about your slow cooker's support and service life by conducting a quick internet search.

It takes careful consideration to strike a balance between functionality, practicality, and aesthetics when choosing the ideal slow cooker. If you pay close attention to the aforementioned criteria, you may ensure a flavorful and seamless slow cooking experience. Thus, equip yourself with the necessary information, trust your culinary intuition, and embark on a flavor-filled adventure!

Chapter 3:
Decoding the Science of Slow Cooking

The tried-and-true cooking method of slow cooking not only makes it simple to have a dinner ready to eat in a short amount of time, but it also offers a variety of other benefits in addition to this major advantage. Cooking is often considered to be both an art and a science due to the fact that it involves combining a broad variety of extremely complex physical and chemical processes in order to produce food that is not only flavorful but also tender. When it is left to boil gently for a substantial amount of time, the food undergoes a number of transformations while it is being cooked. But what exactly are these transformations? How exactly do the flavors develop, and what sorts of nutritional advantages can we anticipate receiving as a result of preparing the meal in this manner? As we make our way further into this chapter, we are going to go even further into the fascinating realm of slow cooking and investigate the mysteries that are hidden within it.

The Magic Behind Prolonged Cooking at Low Temperatures

The process of preparing food over a lengthy period of time at a low temperature is referred to as "slow cooking." The temperature during this method of preparation is often kept in the range of 170 degrees Fahrenheit (77 degrees Celsius) to 280 degrees Fahrenheit (138 degrees Celsius). When compared to other methods of preparation, such as frying or grilling, which only subject the food to high heat for a little length of time before removing it from the heat, this method cooks the food for a greater amount of time over the course of its preparation. The low and slow method is distinguishable from other approaches thanks to a variety of distinct qualities, including the following:

1. **Collagen Breakdown**: The progressive disintegration of collagen is a key contributor to the gradual softening of meat that occurs throughout the process of slow cooking, which is one of the most essential components that plays a role in this process. Connective tissues are known to contain the protein collagen, which has a very hard structure and can be found there. This collagen will, in the end, change into gelatin, which will result in a surface that is smoother as well as a mouthfeel that is richer and more satisfying.
2. **Less Water Loss**: The rate at which water evaporates from food is slowed down by low temperatures, which in turn allows food to retain a greater amount of its moisture. This suggests that foods have a tendency to maintain a higher level of moisture and flavor when they are cooked at a lower temperature for a greater amount of time.
3. **Maillard Reaction and Caramelization**: If the cooking process is slowed down enough, the Maillard reaction and caramelization can still take place even at these lower temperatures. The procedure only requires additional time and moves along in a more methodical fashion. These chemical reactions are responsible for the browning

and development of a flavorful crust that occurs on meat, as well as the development of a sweet flavor in vegetables that have been caramelized. Additionally, these reactions are responsible for the browning and development of a flavorful crust that occurs on vegetables.
4. **Even Heat Distribution**: Because the temperature is lower and the Cook Time is longer, the heat is able to enter the food more evenly, which leads to more uniform cooking.

Benefits For Nutrition and Flavor Enhancement

Not only does cooking food at a low temperature for a considerable length of time make it taste better, but it also helps to preserve a greater quantity of the dish's original nutrients. Slow cooking serves more than just this goal; another one is to achieve the ideal texture in the food.

1. **Flavor Development**: As food cooks slowly, flavors merge and deepen. This is especially true for recipes that contain a number of different ingredients, such as stews and braises, in which each component contributes to the overall complexity of the flavor profile.
2. **Nutrient Retention**: It is a common misconception, but cooking anything slowly can really help maintain some of the food's nutritious worth. Slow cooking, which typically requires less water than boiling or steaming, and lower overall temperatures, may result in a reduction in the amount of nutrients that are lost in comparison to cooking methods that make use of higher temperatures. Heat-sensitive vitamins, such as vitamin C and certain B vitamins, are destroyed by high temperatures.
3. **Enhanced Digestibility**: It's possible that the body will have an easier time digesting foods that have been cooked more slowly. When food is cooked for a longer period of time, the tougher proteins and longer

fibers in it become softer and more easily digestible by the digestive enzymes that are produced by our bodies.

4. **Fat Rendering**: When meat is cooked at a low temperature for an extended period of time, the fat can be rendered away, resulting in a dish that has significantly less oil. After that, you can get rid of the liquid fat by skimming it off the top of the dish if you want to make the dish healthier.

The cooking process that involves using a low heat incorporates aspects of both art and science in its execution. Because of this, we are able to transform ordinary ingredients into exceptional recipes that are nuanced, rich in flavor, and abundant in nutrients. The more we learn about the science that drives this technique, the better we will be able to properly appreciate the alchemy that takes place in our saucepans and slow cookers.

Chapter 4:
Slow Cooker Vs. Crock-Pot

The slow cooker is the generic name for an appliance that brings food to safe temperatures by utilizing heating components that are distributed all around the insert of the device. The term "warming elements" refers to these many types of heating components. The Crock-Pot registered trademark is used to distinguish slow cookers produced by the Rival company from those produced by other companies. Slow cookers can be divided into two categories: those that are not Crock-Pots and those that are. There are many different brands of slow cookers, but some of the most well-known ones are All-Clad, Cuisinart, and Hamilton Beach.

When searching for a slow cooker, it is crucial to bear in mind that there are several kitchen appliances on the market that are marketed to as slow cookers but just have a heating element on the bottom of the appliance. These slow cookers should not be confused with actual slow cookers. When compared to those devices that have heating elements all around the insert, those that only have heating elements on the bottom of the insert take significantly longer to heat the food. The cooking of large quantities of meat in a slow cooker of this type is not suggested by the experts (although it works for soups and stews). When you decide to get a slow cooker, be sure that the model you choose is an authentic one and that it has heating components that surround the insert in every direction.

What Distinguishes a Crock Pot From a Slow Cooker?

The term "crock pot" refers to a particular kind of slow cooker. Both crock pots and slow cookers are essentially the same thing on the inside; they both include a heating element, a lid, and a pot, and they both have the same external appearance. Beans were the only thing that were ever intended to be cooked in a crock pot when it was first invented; but, as it evolved over the course of its history, its capabilities grew to include the ability to cook a broad variety of things. Crock pot was originally the name of a specific brand of slow cooker, but over the years, it has become more generic and can now be used to refer to any kind of slow cooker. To be more specific, the word "crock pot" is now generally used to refer to any form of slow cooker that incorporates a ceramic pot within the heating mechanism. This is because the "crock pot" was the first slow cooker to use the ceramic pot.

One of the many ways in which the crock pot and the slow cooker are related is the fact that both of them have a structure that makes it possible for them to seal in the aroma of the food while it is being cooked inside the pot.

What Each Function Means

A slow cooker variant known as a crock pot is also available. Both the slow cooker and the crock pot have a heating section, a pot, and a lid on the exterior of the device. Both also have the same basic shape. Crock pots were first designed to make the cooking of beans easier; however, over the course of time, they evolved into the multifunctional kitchen equipment that they are today. The original goal of the crock pot was to facilitate the cooking of beans. Before it was later adopted for use in a broader sense, the phrase "crock pot" was originally a brand name of slow cooker that was the subject of its original usage. To be more precise, the word "crock pot" is now generally used to designate any form of slow cooker that use a heating unit that is constructed of ceramic. This is the most common type of slow cooker.

Both the crock pot and the slow cooker have a number of design characteristics, such as the capacity to lock in the flavor of the food and prevent air from leaking out of the container while it is being cooked.

If you select this function, the lid of the cooker will not be needed to cover the food while it is being cooked for you in the browning and sautéing mode because the food will not be covered. You can activate the browning function by pressing this button twice; you can activate the simmering function by pressing the sauté function, adjusting the button twice, and then pressing it again.

Keep the food Warm/Cancel — If you select this function, you will be able to cancel the effect of the function that you had just selected or simply shut off electricity to your Crock Pot Express.

As the name suggests, the Meat/Stew function is used specifically for the purpose of cooking meat and stew. The texture of the meat that is produced by the cooker may be set to be whatever the user desires by modifying the length of time that the meat is allowed to cook for.

Poultry is the feature that allows you to prepare chicken and turkey meat in addition to any other MEAT/STEW meal. You can also use it to prepare any other meal. You have the ability to adjust the desired pressure level as well as the amount of time that the food will be cooked based on your preferences or the requirements listed in the recipe that you are following. Both of these adjustments can be made using the dials on the control panel of the pressure cooker.

If you plan on preparing rice in any form, you should make sure that this function is set before beginning the cooking process. Rice will be cooked by the cooker on its own under a low pressure; the amount of time required for the cooking process will be dictated by the amount of water that you poured into the pot. The rice will be cooked by the cooker.

This option is great for steaming vegetables or seafood, and it works even better when used in conjunction with the quick pressure releasing feature, which helps keep food from being overcooked. Steaming is a healthy alternative to boiling or frying food, and it can be done in the Instant Pot (which can happen if you let your Crock Pot Express release its pressure naturally).

This particular function is necessary for the preparation of soups and broths, so be sure you have it before you start. You can manually modify the length of time required for cooking by selecting the "Adjust" option from the menu (it all depends on how you want your soups, or based on your recipe).

Beans and Chili: The Crock-Pot Express Pressure Cooker comes with a feature that enables you to produce the best beans and chili possible. This feature is included with the pressure cooker. The timer on the slow cooker may be manually adjusted from thirty to forty minutes, and this range is available to you depending on how you like your chili or beans cooked..

Chapter 5:
The Benefits of Slow Cooking

Even if a number of individuals may have gushed to you about how fantastic a crockpot is, it's possible that you've never given any consideration to purchasing one for your own usage. When you have a high-quality brand of crockpot, you will find that all of your greatest fantasies regarding cooking are able to be achieved, and this is a really exciting discovery. You would not have to put yourself through the discomfort of standing in front of a hot stove for an extended amount of time and cooking after a long day at work if you had this option available to you. Imagine what a treat it would be to go into a home that smelled like a chicken that had been braised for hours or salmon that had been seasoned with fresh herbs. That most unquestionably embodies the very essence of what it means to be in heaven, doesn't it? Because of this, not only will you be able to create meals that are wholesome but also nutritious, but as a result, you will also be able to spend less time in front of the stove.

After taking in all of this information, you are probably working under the idea that there is nothing else for you to accomplish at this point. This is a perfectly reasonable assumption to make. You will, however, need to put in a little bit of extra effort in order to be able to take advantage of a variety of meals that are beneficial for both your health and your physique. Before adding the meat and veggies to the slow cooker, it is possible that you will first need to brown the steak in a skillet, and then you will need to dice the vegetables. After you have finished all of the preparation, the last thing you need to do before moving on with the rest of your day is to place all of the vegetables and other ingredients into the slow cooker. After this, you are free to proceed with the rest of your day. When you reach home, there will already be a delicious lunch prepared for you to eat.

One of the many advantages of utilizing a slow cooker is that the dish can be prepared in a short amount of time and will then be ready to be served. In the event that the meal is ready earlier than you anticipated, you will see that the crockpot has switched to the warm mode and has correctly preserved the quality of the food in accordance with the situation. Let's take a look at some additional advantages that come along with using a slow cooker.

Delicious and Nutritious meals

All of the ingredients are freshly prepared, and the cooking process is carried out at a low temperature and for a protracted period of time. Because the vegetables and other components are cooked gently, as well as because they are not subjected to an excessive amount of heat, the nutrients that are present in these components will be preserved. This will ensure that the dish has a high nutritional value. In addition, each and every one of the fluids that are found inside the vegetables will be kept, which will ensure that the dish is more succulent and scrumptious than before.

Saves Time

When you cook using a stovetop, it will take you a considerable amount of time to ensure that the food you are preparing is cooked to the required level of doneness. This is because stovetop cooking requires more direct heat than other methods of cooking. If, on the other hand, you use a slow cooker, you won't have to worry about any of this because the only preparation work that will be required of you is the work to get the slow cooker going in the first place. The slow cooker will finish the cooking for you and take care of everything else while you can focus on other things. You are free to proceed in the manner that is customary for you given the circumstances.

Always useful

You won't ever have to second-guess yourself about whether or not it's the appropriate time to put dinner in the slow cooker because the items that may be prepared in a crockpot are adaptable to any season. You are free to put these household appliances to use whenever the inclination strikes you. Cooking in a crockpot eliminates the need to use an oven, which in turn minimizes the amount of heat that is generated inside of your home as a result of cooking. This is one of the advantages of using a crockpot.

Lesser Energy Consumption

You will discover that using a crockpot takes a noticeably smaller amount of the resource that is known as energy when compared to the utilization of an electric oven.

Very Easy to Clean

You will just need to clean the cutting board, a knife, and potentially the pan that you used to brown the meat that you will be cooking. This is all that will be required of you. This will be the only thing that is expected of you. In addition to that, the slow cooker will be the only object that needs to be cleaned, as opposed to the fact that you will need to clean a variety of various utensils.

Portable

It is not difficult to relocate the food that is contained within a crockpot. It is not necessary to set the meal on a serving plate before eating it if you do not like to do so. You are free to ignore this requirement. This will be handled on your behalf.

When shopping for a slow cooker, you should never, under any circumstances, neglect to take into consideration the number of people who will be eating the food that is prepared in the slow cooker. You will be able to prepare several dishes that are genuinely mouthwatering by utilizing a slow cooker. Bear in mind that in addition to this, you are responsible for properly maintaining your slow cooker. Let's have a look at some pointers that can come in handy when you're using a crockpot to prepare your meals, shall we?

Crockpot Uses, Tips and Tricks

Both crockpots and slow cookers refer to the same category of countertop cooking appliance that cooks food by maintaining a low temperature throughout the process. As a result of this, you will be able to prepare your meals a number of hours before you actually eat them. In addition to being used for the preparation of soups and stews, slow cookers (also known as crockpots) can also be used to cook a wide range of other items, including but not limited to casseroles, roasts, and sweets.

Understanding how to use a slow cooker is not very difficult. The only thing required of you is to put the ingredients in the machine and then select the proper setting so that it will begin to cook the meal in a gentle manner. The food that is being prepared by this innovative piece of cookware is kept at temperatures ranging from 710 degrees Celsius to 740 degrees Celsius throughout the process. The heating element in the slow cooker keeps the temperature stable during the cooking process, which enables the food to be prepared over a more extended period of time. Condensation is generated on the inside of the crockpot due to the fact that the lid does not allow air to leave, which enables the slow cooker to distribute heat more effectively. Because of this, using a crockpot to prepare meals does not require a significant amount of liquid, which is another perk of doing so. In addition, the enzymes and nutrients that are naturally contained in the food are able to be retained since the temperature of the meal is maintained at a level that is lower than the point at which water boils.

Using the Crockpot

Crockpots are ubiquitous kitchen appliances that provide a variety of benefits due to their superiority in the cooking of meat cuts that are less expensive and more difficult to prepare than other types of cuts. In addition, because the food is cooked at a temperature that is reasonable, it does not catch fire at any point throughout the process of cooking, which enables the meal to maintain its robust flavor. But could you walk me through the steps of using the slow cooker? The information that follows is a list of helpful tips about the utilization of slow cookers.

- If you fill the crockpot with more liquid than half or three quarters of its capacity, you will need to add an additional hour to the overall Cook Time. This is because the food will need to be heated for a longer period of time if there is an excessive amount of liquid. If you fill the crockpot with more liquid than half or three quarters of its capacity, you will need to add an additional hour.
- Items that are placed toward the bottom of the container will complete cooking more quickly and keep more moisture than foods that are placed higher up since they will be submerged in the liquid.

To create a dinner that will make your mouth wet, begin by placing meat or root vegetables in the bottom of the dish.

- Before commencing the cooking process, it is essential to remove the skin and any excess fat that may have accumulated. If you proceed in this manner, the food will not have adequate time to cook properly.
- Never in the name of safety lift the lid to check the temperature of the food inside the container. The problem is that if you repeatedly remove the lid, you will lose some of the heat that is necessary to properly cook the meal, which will require you to cook it for a longer period of time. Additional twenty minutes have been granted.

Tips and Tricks

Because the crockpot can be used to prepare such a wide range of dishes, there are some general criteria that you should be familiar with if you want to be able to cook any kind of food properly using your crockpot. When preparing meals using a slow cooker, it is important to keep in mind the helpful advice and suggestions that are provided in the following paragraphs.

- Before moving on, make sure that any ground meats have any excess fat rendered off of them by first cooking them in a skillet. This will not only give the meat an additional taste, but it will also remove any excess fat that might otherwise slow down the cooking process.
- If you want to avoid giving the dish a rubbery flavor, add the fish during the final hour of cooking rather than earlier in the process. If you bake it for an extended amount of time, it will change texture and become rubbery.
- Before being placed in a slow cooker to finish cooking, substantial quantities of meat should be browned in a skillet first so that the finished product has an enhanced flavor.

- When adding the tender vegetables to the dish, wait until the last 45 minutes of cooking time before doing so. This will avoid the vegetables from becoming overcooked.
- When using dairy products, particularly milk and cream, it is preferable to hold off until the very end of the cooking process. If you cook the dairy products for an excessive amount of time, the milk will curdle, which is the separation of the milk's protein from its natural water content. This occurs when the milk is heated to temperatures that are over its normal boiling point.

Chapter 6:
FAQs

Slow cookers, which are most frequently identified with the brand name "Crock-Pot" due to their widespread use, have been a common fixture on kitchen countertops for a significant number of years. In spite of the wide range of applications they have, a significant number of mysteries remain surround how they perform their functions. Now that we have your attention, let's go into some of the most serious worries that you may have had in the past but were probably too bashful to discuss.

Can you leave a Crock-Pot on while no one is home without risk?

Slow cookers, most notably those sold under the "Crock-Pot" brand, have been a fixture on kitchen countertops for a long time. Despite their widespread use, there are still a lot of unanswered mysteries about how they operate. Now that we have your focus, let's discuss some of the most important issues you may have been afraid to bring up.

Does it matter if the recipe requires a slow cooker of a different size?

Size matters, it's true, but not always in the way you may think. Using a Crock-Pot larger than recommended could result in your dinner cooking faster and the food drying out because of the larger surface area. Conversely, an overfilled cooker may result in an uneven cooking pattern. A generally sound rule of thumb? Before putting your slow cooker on, fill it to about half to three quarters of the way to the top for the best results.

Can you use a Crock-Pot with frozen [fill in the blank?

Although it is possible to use frozen components in a recipe, doing so presents a number of challenges. The Cook Time may need to be extended if frozen ingredients are used, which may also result in dishes that are not cooked uniformly. But if you're in a bind, simply keep in mind that you'll need some additional time and maybe a pinch of patience as well.

Can a Crock-Pot be used in the oven? Maybe over a stove?

While some daring individuals may find them appealing, Crock-Pots aren't meant to be used with ovens or stoves. While ceramic inserts work great for low-temperature cooking, abrupt temperature swings might cause them to break. Keep your attention on the task at hand to avoid getting into a messy scenario.

Will you get food poisoning if you place a chicken stew in the Crock-Pot when you leave for work and set the timer for 4 hr. later?

I mean, who could resist coming home to a pot of stew simmering on the stove? However, if raw ingredients—especially chicken—are kept at room temperature for an extended amount of time, it's a surefire way for germs to grow. To lower the chance of a culinary catastrophe, it is best practice to start cooking as soon as the ingredients have been put in the cooking area.

If your job requires you to work a regular 8-hr. day, how do you manage it?

It is true that most recipes take between four and eight hours to complete, don't they? A possible solution to this issue is a Crock-Pot that may be programmed to include a "keep warm" option. You may be sure that your supper will be hot without being overdone because the appliance will just keep the food warm until you return.

Can you prepare rice or pasta in a Crock-Pot?

Absolutely! Although not the most common items for slow cooking, rice and pasta can still benefit from the warmth supplied by a Crock-Pot. Just make sure there is enough liquid, and be prepared to experiment with the timings until the right consistency is reached.

Do slow cookers fit in the dishwasher?

A lot of the slow cookers available now have removable ceramic inserts that can be washed in the dishwasher on a regular basis. But be sure to thoroughly review the instructions provided by the manufacturer. But, as the electrical base could be harmed, you should never place it in the dishwasher or sink. All that's needed is a fast wipe off.

How should a Crock-Pot be transported?

Bringing the best dish you've ever made for a group dinner? Verify that the lid is securely attached. Certain variations are pre-installed with lockable lids for easier transportation. You can use bungee cords or place the cooker in a box to provide additional stability while it is being carried.

So now you know the solution! An in-depth explanation of some of the more subtle features of the slow cooker, the kitchen tool that everyone loves to use. Cheers to many more hours of easily prepared and delicious dinners!

Chapter 7: Breakfast Recipes

1. Apple Crumble Breakfast Pudding

- Serves 6

Ingredients

Pudding

- salt 1 pinch
- 5 large apples, sliced – do not peel!
- almond milk 1 C.
- cornstarch 2 tbsp.
- crushed cinnamon 1 tsp.
- water 2 C.
- maple syrup 2 tbsp.
- ½ C. chia seeds

Cinnamon Crunch Topping

- blanched almond flour ½ C
- For serving: raisins, nuts, almond milk
- unsweetened shredded coconut
- pure vanilla extract 1 tsp.
- coconut sugar ¼ C. ¼ C.
- 1 tsp. cinnamon
- ¼ C. unsweetened apple sauce

Directions

1. Place the almond milk, water, maple syrup, chia seeds, cornstarch, cinnamon, and salt in the bottom of a 3-quart slow cooker.
2. Place the diced apples on top without mixing them.
3. Mix the ingredients for the crisp topping in a large bowl. Distribute them evenly between the apples. Cook on LOW for 2–4 hours.
4. Turn off the slow cooker and let it sit for one hour.
5. If desired, garnish with almond milk, almonds, and raisins. Enjoy!

Nutrition Info: KCal 363, Fat 21.5 g, Carbs 49.3 g, Protein 3.8 g

2. Honey Sweet Raisin Bread

- Serves 6-8

Ingredients

- 1 ⅓ C. lukewarm water
- 1 tbsp. honey
- 2 tsp. fast rising dried yeast

- 4 C. bread flour
- 1 tsp. salt
- ½ C. raisins, previously soaked and drained for softness

Directions

1. Mix honey, water, and yeast together. Before putting the mixture away, let it a few minutes to bubble.
2. Combine the flour and salt in a bowl. Make a well in the center.
3. Pour half of the yeast mixture into the well. Using a fork, stir the mixture until it starts to get sticky.
4. Add the leftover yeast mixture to the flour. Mix to form a dough.
5. Knead the dough for about 5 minutes, or until it is smooth, on a surface dusted with flour.
6. Add the raisins to the dough and spread them throughout.
7. Roll the dough into a ball after dusting it with flour.
8. Place a piece of parchment paper in the slow cooker's bottom.
9. Put the dough in the slow cooker's center. When cooking, fold the parchment away from the dough to prevent sticking.
10. Cook on HIGH for one to two hours, checking the meal every thirty minutes after the first hour.
11. When the crust is golden brown and a little tap produces a hollow sound, the bread is done. The interior temperature can also be measured. A thermometer with an instant readout should read 190 ºF.
12. Cool before slicing.

Nutrition Info: KCal 71, Fat 1.1 g, Carbs 13.6 g, Protein 2.0 g

3. Silky Smooth Hot Chocolate

- Serves 8-10

Ingredients

- Unsweetened cocoa powder, 1/4 cup
- Whole milk, 6 C.
- Heavy whipping cream, 2 cups
- 1 can of sweetened condensed milk, 14 oz.
- Semisweet chocolate chips, 2 C.

Directions

1. Combine all of the ingredients in a slow cooker.
2. Cook, covered, on LOW for two hours.
3. While cooking, stir occasionally with a whisk. Ensure that all of the chocolate has melted and been well mixed into the recipe.
4. If desired, present miniature marshmallows (optional).

Nutrition Info: KCal 587, Fat 35 g, Carbs 58 g, Protein 16 g

4. Sweet Morning Chocolate Rice Pudding

- Serves 2

Ingredients

- ¾ C. evaporated milk
- packed brown sugar ⅔ C.
- ½ C. unsweetened cocoa powder
- water 4 ½ C
- ½ C. long grain rice, uncooked

Directions

1. Put the evaporated milk aside.
2. the items that are left in the slow cooker.
3. Mix until thoroughly combined.
4. Cook covered for 5 to 6 hours on LOW or HIGH.
5. Pour some evaporated milk on top and serve hot or cold.

Nutrition Info: KCal 195, Fat 7.6 g, Carbs 30 g, Protein 4.3 g

5. Baked Beans with Wedges

- Serves 2

Ingredients

- canned cannellini beans, 2 C.
- 2 C. Vegetable or chicken broth
- 1 thinly sliced onion,

- 2 thick-cut bacon strips,
- 1 tablespoon sugar
- a half-cup of tomato paste
- ¼ cup of canned diced green chilies
- 2 cups of diced tomatoes

For the potato wedges:

- 1 tbsp. white flour
- ¼ tsp. cayenne pepper, more if you like very spicy
- 1 tbsp. mixed herbs
- Enough pepper & salt
- 2 baking potatoes, cut into 8 pieces
- 2 tbsp. oil

Directions

1. While the oven preheats to 400°F, make the potato wedges.
2. In a medium bowl, combine the flour, herbs, and cayenne. Season the food with salt and pepper to taste.
3. Mix the oil and potatoes together well with the coating. Bake for 35 minutes, or until cooked through and crispy.
4. To the slow cooker, add the beans, 2 cups of broth, onion, bacon, sugar, tomato paste, tomatoes, and chiles.
5. Cover and cook on HIGH for three hours.
6. Turn the slow cooker down to LOW and add the potatoes. Cook for a another hour.

Nutrition Info: KCal 399, Fat 11 g, Carbs 60 g, Protein 19 g

6. Honey Granola and Blueberry Yogurt

- Serves 4-8

Ingredients

- 8 C. milk
- ½ C. yogurt starter or live yogurt
- Honey Granola
- Blueberries
- Honey

Directions

1. The slow cooker should be on LOW. Add the milk.
2. Cook on LOW for 2 hours and 12 minutes. This slow cooker takes up to 2 quarts, so increase the Cook Time by 15 minutes.
3. After 2 ½ hours, unplug the cooker. After three hours, leave the pot covered and let the milk cool.
4. After the three hours are up, place 12 C. of the warmed milk in a small bowl. Add the live yogurt starter and stir until fully combined.
5. Stir and return the contents to the crock.
6. Put the cover back. Cover the saucepan with a blanket or two heavy cloths.
7. Let stand for ten to twelve hours.
8. Pour the yogurt into a cheesecloth-lined colander if it is thick. Till the required thickness is reached, strain. Straining About a quart is served.
9. Stir. Put the container in the fridge. It has a maximum of seven days.
10. For every cup of yogurt, top with ¼ cup of blueberries and granola and serve chilled after sweetened with honey.

Nutrition Info: KCal 120, Fat 3 g, Carbs 21 g, Protein 2 g

7. Fruity and Spiced Butter Spread

- Serves 8-16

Ingredients

- freshly crushed nutmeg ¼ tsp 4 pounds mixed fresh fruit (such as pears, apples, cherries, plums, or peaches), stripped, pitted and cored
- ¼ – ½ C. water
- pure vanilla extract 1 tbsp.
- crushed cinnamon ¼ tsp.
- .
- ½ to1 C. sugar (you may also use honey or maple syrup)

Directions

1. Fruit that is to be put in the slow cooker should be uniformly sliced into bite-sized pieces.
2. Cook on LOW for 2 hours, stirring now and again.
3. After adding water, cook for a further 16 hours. To achieve a thicker consistency, you can simmer the food for an additional 14 to 15 hours with the lid partially open.
4. Transfer to a food processor or blender after 16 hours to purée. Another option is a handheld blender.
5. Return the liquid to the slow cooker. Stir in sugar, nutmeg, cinnamon, and vanilla.
6. Continue cooking on LOW for a further two hours with the cover cracked, or until the consistency is ideal.

7. Spoon into jars. Chill and store in the refrigerator.

Nutrition (per tbsp.): KCal 31, Fat 0 g, Carbs 7.7 g, Protein 0.1 g

8. Slow Cooked Cinnamon Applesauce

- Serves 12

Ingredients

- 6 pounds of apples, sliced after being cored and stripped
- Apple juice, 1 cup
- lemon juice from one
- ½ C. brown sugar
- 1 tsp. cinnamon

Directions

1. Add all of the ingredients to the slow cooker.
2. Cover and cook on HIGH for 4 hours, stirring periodically.
3. Switch off the slow cooker once the appropriate consistency is reached.
4. Store in an airtight jar in the refrigerator.

Nutrition Info: KCal 149, Fat 1 g, Carbs 38 g, Protein 1 g

9. Easy Bacon and Egg Casserole

- Serves 6-8

Ingredients

- 8 slices pre-cooked bacon
- 1 bell pepper, diced
- 1 onion, diced
- 12 eggs
- 1 C. whole milk
- Enough black pepper and salt
- Cooking Spray

Directions

1. Apply cooking spray inside the pot to make it ready.
2. Whisk the eggs, milk, pepper, and salt together in a bowl.
3. Simmer the onion and bell pepper in a pan over medium heat for 2 to 3 minutes, or until fragrant. Remove from the heat source and allow to cool for a bit.
4. Add a little onion, bell pepper, and bacon to the eggs.
5. The beaten eggs should be added to the slow cooker.
6. Cook the eggs for 6 to 8 hours, or until they are set, on LOW heat in the oven.

Nutrition Info: KCal 564, Fat 132 g, Carbs 13.2 g, Protein 156 g

10. Maple and Blueberry Steel Cut Oatmeal

- Serves 6 to 8

Ingredients

- Cooking spray
- 2 C. of steel cut oats (don't replace with any other type of oats)
- pure maple syrup ¼ C.
- 6-8 C. of water (increase for smoother consistency, if desired)
- ½ tsp. salt
- light brown sugar ¼ C.
- dried blueberries ¾ C.
- cinnamon 1 tsp.

Directions

1. Give the oven or stove a good spraying.
2. Stir everything together in the slow cooker.
3. Cook on LOW for 7 to 8 hours with the lid on.
4. Give it one last vigorous stir and serve right away.
5. If kept in an airtight container in the refrigerator, leftovers can last for three to four days.

Nutrition Info: KCal 160, Fat 2.5 g, Carbs 32 g, Protein 4 g

11. Cinnamon-Raisin French Toast Breakfast

- Serves 6

Ingredients

- ½ C. packed light brown sugar
- 7 large eggs
- whole milk 2 ½ C.
- Non-stick cooking spray
- 16 cinnamon-raisin bread slices, cubed
- heavy cream 1 C.
- 2 C. pecans or walnuts (optional)

Directions

1. To stop food from sticking, cover your slow cooker with foil and give it a quick coat of nonstick spray.
2. Put the bread cubes inside the slow cooker.
3. Whisk together the sugar, cream, eggs, and milk (2 C. of pecan or walnuts, optional).
4. Pour the egg mixture over the bread in a slow cooker, pressing down slightly to allow the bread to absorb the liquid.
5. Cover and cook on low heat for four hours (or HIGH for 2 hr.).
6. Remove the slow cooker's lid, turn it off, and let it to cool for fifteen minutes.
7. Serve.

Nutrition Info: KCal 149, Fat 7 g, Carbs 16 g, Protein 5 g

12. Lavender Infused Blueberry Jam

- Serves 10-15

Ingredients

- 10 C. fresh or frozen blueberries
- 2 tsp. culinary lavender
- 2 C. sugar
- 1 tsp. lemon zest
- ½ tsp. nutmeg powder (optional)
- ¼ C. water

Directions

1. Put the blueberries and water in your covered slow cooker, then simmer on LOW for one hour.
2. After an hour, take off the cover and cook for a further four hours on LOW.
3. After adding the sugar, lemon zest, and lavender, check the consistency.
4. Remove the lid and cook on HIGH for an additional hour or until the desired consistency is achieved for richer blueberry butter.
5. Puree using a handheld blender until it's smooth.
6. Keep refrigerated in an airtight container.

Nutrition Info: KCal 35, Fat 0 g, Carbs 9 g, Protein 0 g

13. Crockpot Oatmeal

- Serves 6

Ingredients

- vegan milk, unsweetened 4 C
- steel cut oats 1 C.
- cinnamon 1 tsp.
- diced nuts ¼ C.
- bananas, ripe, sliced 1–2
- maple syrup ½ C.

Optional

- ½ C. carob chips
- 1 tbsp. crushed flax seeds
- 2 tbsp. almond butter

Directions

1. Apply some oil to the slow cooker's walls. In a slow cooker, combine all the ingredients except the carob chips; stir until well mixed. Cook the oats for 6 to 8 hours on low heat. If you'd like, incubate it overnight.
2. Warm up and serve. Add nut butter, cinnamon, maple syrup, or carob chips on top.

Nutrition Info: KCal 523, Fat 37 g, Carbs 49 g, Protein 8 g

14. Vegan Pumpkin Spice Syrup

- Serves 4

Ingredients

- 2 cans full-fat coconut milk
- packed light brown sugar 2 C.
- organic pumpkin purée 2 C.
- crushed cinnamon 1 tsp.
- crushed ginger 1 tsp
- crushed cardamom ¼ tsp.
- crushed allspice ¼ tsp
- Pinch of cloves

Directions

1. In a slow cooker, combine the coconut milk, brown sugar, pumpkin puree, and spices (cinnamon, ginger, cardamom, cloves, and allspice). After mixing with a whisk, reduce heat to LOW and simmer for 7 hours.
2. After the Cook Time is over, use a whisk to combine all the ingredients and break up any bits that may still be in the syrup.
3. Can be kept in the refrigerator for a week.

Nutrition Info: KCal 33, Fat 0 g, Carbs 7 g, Protein 0 g

15. Strawberry French Toast

- Serves 2

Ingredients

- 1 tsp. butter, melted
- 2 medium-sized eggs
- ½ C. 2% milk
- 1 tsp. vanilla extract
- ⅛ tsp. sea salt
- 4 cut into 1-inch cubes Whole grain bread, crusts removed
- 2 C. strawberries
- 2 oz. low-fat cream cheese, cut in small chunks

Directions

1. Cover the entire interior of the slow cooker with butter.
2. In a large bowl, thoroughly mix together the eggs, milk, vanilla, and salt.
3. Toss the bread cubes with the egg and set aside so they can absorb the flavor for three to four minutes.
4. Pour half of the bread mixture into the slow cooker. As a garnish, you can use whipped topping and strawberries.
5. Cover with the remaining bread crumbs.
6. Cook, covered, on HIGH for 2 1/2 hours or LOW for 6 hours.
7. Spoon into separate bowls or onto separate plates, and enjoy!

Nutrition Info: KCal 389, Fat 10.2 g, Carbs 40.3 g, Protein 17 g

16. Sweet Cinnamon Swirled Pancake

Serves 2

Ingredients

- Cooking spray
- 1 C. of biscuit or pancake mix
- 1 tbsp. cinnamon
- ½ C. milk
- 1 egg
- ⅓ C. of granulated sugar

Directions

1. Get enough of cooking spray ready for the slow cooker's bottom.
2. In a large mixing dish, whisk together the egg, milk, and baking mix. To the slow cooker, add.
3. In a separate bowl, mix the cinnamon and sugar together. Top the prepared batter with this addition. Using a spatula or spoon handle, swirl in the sugar and cinnamon mixture.
4. On HIGH, cook for about 1 hour to 1 hour and 15 minutes.
5. A fork inserted in the center of the pancake should come out clean.

Nutrition Info: KCal 194, Fat 2.7 g, Carbs 16.5 g, Protein 2.2 g

17. Vegan Omelet

- Serves 2

Ingredients

- 2 tbsp. nutritional yeast
- ½ tsp. turmeric
- silken tofu 1 C.
- garlic 2 cloves
- ½ bell pepper, diced
- ½ tomato, diced
- paprika ½ tsp.
- ½ C. mushrooms, sliced
- ½ C. vegan cheddar
- Salt and pepper

Directions

1. In a food processor, combine the tofu, nutritional yeast, garlic, and seasonings; process until smooth. Blend the mixture using a blender or blenders until it's smooth. It could need a tablespoon or two of water.
2. Pour the mixture into the slow cooker and stir in the cheese and vegetables.
3. For one hour, heat on high with a cover on, monitoring periodically to make sure the tofu and vegetables are cooked through.

Nutrition Info: KCal 356, Fat 16 g, Carbs 29 g, Protein 16 g

18. Healthy Oats and Quinoa Breakfast

- Serves 6

Ingredients

- Cooking spray
- 1 ½ C. of steel cut oats (don't replace with any other type of oats)
- ½ C. quinoa (rinsed)
- 4 tbsp. brown sugar
- 2 tbsp. pure maple syrup
- 1 ½ tsp. vanilla extract
- ¼ tsp. salt
- 4 ½ C. of water
- Optional: fresh berries, 'extra sugar for topping

Directions

1. Give the oven or stove a good spraying.
2. Add all the ingredients to the slow cooker and stir to mix well.
3. Cook for 6 hours on LOW with a lid on. (Cooking it for longer than six hours may result in mush.)
4. The oats should be taken off the fire and put in a different container after 6 hours.
5. Top with your preferred topping as soon as you can.

Nutrition Info: KCal 343, Fat 9.8 g, Carbs 58.3 g, Protein 10.4 g

19. Oats with Quinoa

- Serves 6

Ingredients

Oatmeal

- 1½ C. steel cut oats, rinsed
- quinoa ½ C.
- ¼ tsp. salt
- 4½ C. water
- brown sugar 4 tbsp.
- maple syrup 2 tbsp.
- 1½ tsp. vanilla extract
- ¼ tsp. crushed cinnamon (optional)
- Non-stick cooking spray

Garnish

- Fresh berries (optional)
- Splash of milk (optional)
- Sugar for topping (optional)

Directions

1. Apply cooking spray to a crockpot to grease it.
2. After combining the remaining ingredients for the oatmeal, pour it into the slow cooker.
3. Cook for 6 to 7 hours on LOW; do not cook anything longer than 7 hours.
4. Spoon into a bowl, garnish with the parsley, and serve.

Nutrition Info: KCal 412, Fat 1 g, Carbs 62 g, Protein 10 g

20. Classic Strawberry Rhubarb Jam

- Serves 30

Ingredients

- 3 pounds fresh strawberries, diced
- 2 pounds rhubarb, diced
- 1 C. of sugar
- ½ tsp. cinnamon

Directions

1. Place alternating layers of rhubarb and strawberry in a slow cooker.
2. A half cup of sugar might help the fruit.
3. Scatter the leftover strawberries and rhubarb over the sugar.
4. Sprinkle the remaining cinnamon and sugar in an even layer over the top.
5. Cook for 4 hours on LOW with a lid on.
6. Remove the lid, thoroughly stir the jam, and cook on LOW for an additional hour. Cook until the desired consistency is achieved.
7. If you want a thick jam, mash it; if you want a smooth jam, mix it.
8. Serve this delicious jam over toast or over yogurt, pancakes, or vanilla ice cream.

Nutrition Info: KCal 50, Fat 0.9 g, Carbs 13 g, Protein 0 g

Chapter 8:
Lunch Recipes

21. Mustard-Crusted Salmon

- Serves: 4
- Prep Time: 3 min.
- Cook Time: 4 hr.

Ingredients

- 4 pieces salmon fillets
- 2 tbsp. stone-crushed mustard
- ¼ C. full sour cream
- enough pepper & salt
- 2 tsp. lemon juice

Directions:

1. To taste, season the salmon fillets with salt and pepper. Add a tiny bit of lemon juice on top.
2. Evenly distribute the crumbled mustard over the fillets.
3. Simmer for two hours on high or four hours on low in a slow cooker.
4. Cover the fish with sour cream one hour prior to Cook Time.
5. Keep cooking the fish until it flakes.

Nutrition Info: KCal: 74; Carbs: 4.2g; Protein: 25.9g; Fat:13.8 g

22. Thai Clear Chicken Soup

- Serves: 8
- Cook Time: 8 hr.

Ingredients

- 1 whole chicken, cut into pieces
- 1 stalk of lemon grass, cut into 5-inches in length
- Juice from 1 lime, freshly squeezed
- 20 fresh basil leaves
- 5 slices of ginger
- Enough pepper & salt

Directions:

1. Place all ingredients into the slow cooker.
2. Close the lid and cook for 6 hours on high or 8 hours on low.
3. Sprinkle cilantro on top.

Nutrition Info: KCal: 236; Carbs: 7.9g; Protein: 23.5g; Fat: 18.6g

23. Easy CrockPot Meatballs

- Serves: 6
- Cook Time: 10 hr.

Ingredients

- 2 tbsp. olive oil
- 1 tbsp. cumin
- 1 tsp. paprika
- 2 pounds crushed beef
- 2 eggs, beaten
- 3 cloves of garlic, minced
- 1 tbsp. dried parsley
- Enough pepper & salt

Directions:

1. Lightly coat the Crock-bottom Pot's with olive oil.
2. Mix everything together in a big bowl.
3. Using your hands, form tiny balls and put them into the CrockPot.
4. Cook, covered, over high heat for 6 hours or low heat for 10 hours.
5. The meatballs should be turned or flipped halfway through the Cook Time.
6. Once the meat is thoroughly cooked, shut the lid and keep cooking.

Nutrition Info: KCal: 413; Carbs: 2.5g; Protein: 46.7g; Fat: 21.4g

24. Turkey Soup with Rosemary and Kale

- Serves: 6
- Cook Time: 8 hr.

Ingredients

- ½ onion, diced
- 1 tbsp. tallow or ghee
- garlic, minced 2 cloves
- Enough pepper & salt
- 1-pound turkey meat, cut into bite-sized pieces
- 4 C. homemade chicken stock
- 2 sprigs rosemary, diced
- 3 C. kale, diced

Directions:

1. Everything save the greens should go into the slow cooker.
2. Close the lid and cook on high for 6 hours or on low for 8 hours.
3. Add the greens one hour before the cooking is done.
4. Once the kale has wilted, cover the pot and cook.

Nutrition Info: KCal: 867; Carbs: 2.6g; Protein: 151.3g; Fat: 23.6g

25. Mustard Garlic Shrimps

- Serves: 4
- Prep Time: 5 min.
- Cook Time: 2 hr. and 30 min.

Ingredients

- 3 tbsp. garlic, minced
- 1-pound shrimp, shelled and deveined
- 1 tsp. olive oil
- 1 tsp. Dijon mustards
- Enough pepper & salt
- Parsley for garnish

Directions:

1. Heat the olive oil in a skillet and sauté the garlic until it becomes aromatic and starts to turn golden.
2. After transferring, add the shrimp and Dijon mustard to the crockpot. Mix well to blend.
3. Add as much pepper and salt as desired.
4. Close the lid and cook for 30 minutes on high or 2 hours on low.
5. After finished, garnish with parsley.

Nutrition Info: KCal: 138; Carbs: 3.2g; Protein: 23.8g; Fat: 2.7g

26. Spicy Basil Shrimp

- Serves: 4
- Prep Time: 3 min.
- Cook Time: 2 hr.

Ingredients

- ¼ C. packed fresh basil leaves
- ¼ tsp. cayenne pepper
- 1-pound raw shrimp, shelled and deveined
- Enough pepper & salt
- 1 tbsp. butter

Directions:

1. Everything is set up in the crock cooker.
2. Stir it around a bit.
3. Close the lid and cook for 30 minutes on high or 2 hours on low.

Nutrition Info: KCal: 236; Carbs: 7.9g; Protein: 23.5g; Fat: 18.6g

27. Express Shrimps and Sausage Jambalaya Stew

- Serves: 4
- Prep Time: 5 min.
- Cook Time: 3 hr.

Ingredients

- 1 tsp. canola oil

- 1 can chicken broth
- 8 oz. shrimps, shelled and deveined
- 8 oz. andouille sausage, cut into slices
- 1 16-oz. bag frozen bell pepper and onion mix

Directions:

1. In a skillet over medium heat, sauté the sausages until the fat renders. Setting apart.
2. Transfer the blend of veggies into the slow cooker.
3. Pour in the chicken broth and add the sausages.
4. Finally, stir in the shrimp.
5. Cook on low for one or three hours, depending on your tastes.

Nutrition Info: KCal: 316; Carbs: 6.3; Protein: 32.1g; Fat: 25.6g

28. Crockpot Chicken Curry

- Serves: 6
- Prep Time: 3 min.
- Cook Time: 8 hr.

Ingredients

-
- 1 can coconut milk
- 2 pounds chicken breasts, bones removed 1 onion, diced
- 4 tbsp. curry powder
- Enough pepper & salt

Directions:

1. Add all ingredients to the slow cooker.
2. Mix thoroughly to blend the components.
3. Close the lid and cook on high for 6 hours or on low for 8 hours.

Nutrition Info: KCal:468; Carbs: 9g; Protein: 34.5g; Fat: 33.7g

29. Five-Spice Tilapia

- Serves: 4
- Prep Time: 3 min.
- Cook Time: 5 hr.

Ingredients

- 4 tilapia fillets
- 3 scallions, thinly sliced
- 1 tsp. Chinese five-spice powder
- 1 tbsp. sesame oil
- ¼ C. gluten-free soy sauce

Directions:

1. Tilapia fillets pair wonderfully with Chinese five spice powder.
2. Put the fish in the crockpot with sesame oil on top.
3. Set the timer for two hours on high or four hours on low.
4. To lightly brown the opposite side, flip the fish halfway through the Cook Time.
5. Add the scallion and soy sauce and continue to cook for an additional hour.

Nutrition Info: KCal: 153; Carbs: 0.9g; Protein: 25.8g; Fat: 5.6g

30. Lemon Parsley Chicken

- Serves: 4
- Prep Time: 5 min.
- Cook Time: 8 hr.

Ingredients

- 1 lemon, sliced thinly
- ½ C. parsley, diced
- 1-pound chicken breasts, bones removed
- Enough pepper & salt
- 2 tbsp. butter, melted

Directions:

1. Put foil along the bottom of the crockpot.
2. Spread melted butter to coat the foil.
3. Season the chicken breasts with salt and pepper to taste.
4. Lay out on the foil, then cover with slices of lemon.
5. Add some chopped parsley on top.
6. It can be cooked for six hours on high or eight hours on low.

Nutrition Info: KCal: 226; Carbs: 7g; Protein: 23g; Fat: 15g

31. Basic Shredded Chicken

- Serves: 12
- Cook Time: 8 hr.

Ingredients

- 4 tbsp. butter
- 6 pounds chicken breasts, bones and skin removed
- 5 C. homemade chicken broth
- 1 tsp. salt
- ½ tsp. black pepper

Directions:

1. Place all ingredients into the slow cooker.
2. Close the lid and cook for 6 hours on high or 8 hours on low.
3. Shed the chicken with two forks.
4. Return to the slow cooker and cook on high for an additional 30 minutes.

Nutrition Info: KCal: 421; Carbs: 0.5g; Protein: 48.1g; Fat: 25.4g

32. CrockPot Fajita Chicken

- Serves: 8
- Cook Time: 8 hr.

Ingredients

- 1 C. roma tomatoes, diced
- Enough pepper & salt
- 2 ½ pounds chicken thighs and breasts, skin and bones removed
- ½ tsp. cumin
- ½ tsp. chipotle pepper, diced
- 1 onion, sliced

- 4 cloves of garlic, minced
- 2 C. bell peppers, sliced
- 1 tsp. crushed coriander

Directions:

1. Place all ingredients into the slow cooker.
2. Close the lid and cook for 6 hours on high or 8 hours on low.
3. Shred the meat from the bird using two forks.
4. Return to the slow cooker and cook on high for an additional 30 minutes.
5. Sprinkle chopped cilantro on top.

Nutrition Info: KCal: 328; Carbs: 3.3g; Protein: 39.5g; Fat: 17.7g

33. Onion and Bison Soup

- Serves: 8
- Cook Time: 10 hr.

Ingredients

- 6 onions, julienned
- 2 pounds bison meat, cubed
- 3 sprigs of thyme
- 1 bay leaf
- Enough pepper & salt
- 2 tbsp. olive oil
- 3 C. beef stock
- ½ C. sherry

Directions:

1. Place all ingredients into the slow cooker.
2. Make a vigorous stir.
3. Cook, covered, over high heat for 8 hours or low heat for 10 hours.

Nutrition Info: KCal: 341; Carbs: 9.5g; Protein: 24.5g; Fat: 21.8g

34. CrockPot Yellow Chicken Curry

- Serves: 5
- Cook Time: 8 hr.

Ingredients

- 1 thumb-size ginger, sliced
- 4 cloves of garlic, minced
- 1 tsp. cinnamon
- 1 ½ pounds boneless chicken breasts, cut into chunks
- 6 C. vegetable broth (made from boiling onions, broccoli, bell pepper, and carrots in 7 C. water)
- 2 tsp. crushed coriander
- 1 tsp. turmeric powder
- 1 C. coconut milk, unsweetened
- ½ tsp. cayenne pepper
- Salt to taste
- 1 C. tomatoes, crushed
- 1 tbsp. cumin

Directions:

1. Throw everything into the slow cooker.
2. Cook on high for 6 hours or low for 8 hours with the lid closed.

Nutrition Info: KCal: 291; Carbs: 6.1g; Protein: 32.5g; Fat: 15.4g

35. Fiesta Pork Chops

- Serves: 4
- Cook Time: 12 hr.

Ingredients

- 2 cloves of garlic, minced
- 1 tsp. chili powder
- ¼ tsp. oregano leaves
- 4 large pork chops, bone in
- Enough pepper & salt
- ½ tbsp. ghee
- 2/3 C. homemade chicken broth
- 1 tbsp. lime juice
- 1/8 C. mild green chilies, diced
- Enough pepper & salt
- ¼ C. fresh cilantro, diced
- ½ onion, diced

Directions:

1. Place everything in the slow cooker, excluding the cilantro.
2. Make a vigorous stir.
3. Close the lid and cook on high for 10 hours or on low for 12 hours.

4. When cooked, sprinkle cilantro on top.

Nutrition Info: KCal: 365; Carbs: 5.1g; Protein: 41.3g; Fat: 19.1g

36. Chipotle Chicken Enchilada Stew

- Serves: 5
- Cook Time: 8 hr.

Ingredients

- 1 ½ pounds chicken breasts, bones and skin removed
- 1 onion, diced
- 4 cloves of garlic, minced
- 1 tbsp. cumin
- 1 green pepper, diced
- 1 tsp. oregano
- Enough pepper & salt
- 1 yellow pepper, diced
- 1 C. tomatoes, diced
- 2 C. homemade chicken stock
- 3 jalapeno peppers, diced
- 2 C. crushed chicken
- 1 tbsp. chili powder
- 1 tbsp. chipotle pepper, diced

Directions:

1. Place all ingredients into the slow cooker.
2. Close the lid and cook for 6 hours on high or 8 hours on low.

3. Add chopped cilantro and sliced avocado as garnish.

Nutrition Info: KCal: 708; Carbs: 9.2g; Protein: 108.4g; Fat: 23.6g

37. Lamb's Feet Soup

- Serves: 8
- Cook Time: 10 hr.

Ingredients

- 1-inch ginger, grated
- 3 cloves of garlic, minced
- 1 ½ pounds lamb's feet
- 1 onion, diced
- 1 C. tomatoes, crushed
- 1 bay leaf
- 4 C. water
- 1 tsp. coriander seeds
- 1 tsp. black peppercorns

Directions:

1. Place all ingredients into the slow cooker.
2. Mix everything well.
3. Cook, covered, over high heat for 8 hours or low heat for 10 hours.

Nutrition Info: KCal: 229; Carbs: 2.4g; Protein: 21.6g; Fat:14.9 g

38. Herb-Crusted Pork Chops

- Serves: 4
- Cook Time: 12 hr.

Ingredients

- parsley flakes 1 tsp.
- 2 tbsp. olive oil
- 4 pork chops
- dried marjoram 1 tsp.
- crushed thyme ½ tsp.
- salt 1/8 tsp.
- 1/8 tsp. black pepper
- ½ C. chicken broth

Directions:

1. Place all ingredients into the slow cooker.
2. Mix everything well.
3. Close the lid and cook on high for 10 hours or on low for 12 hours.

Nutrition Info: KCal: 436; Carbs: 0.4g; Protein: 46.7g; Fat: 26.2g

39. Herbed Pork Tenderloin

- Serves: 6
- Cook Time: 12 hr.

Ingredients

- 2 pork tenderloins, skin removed
- 2 tbsp. ginger, grated
- 1 tsp. salt
- ½ tsp. crushed black pepper
- ½ C. cilantro, diced
- 3 green onions, diced
- ½ C. extra virgin olive oil
- ½ C. apple cider vinegar
- ½ tsp. all spice
- 1/8 tsp. crushed cloves
- 2 jalapeno peppers, diced

Directions:

1. After combining all the ingredients in a bowl, marinate the meat for at least two hours in the refrigerator.
2. Line the Crock-bottom Pot's with aluminum foil.
3. Fold up the meat.
4. Close the lid and cook on high for 10 hours or on low for 12 hours.

Nutrition Info: KCal: 253; Carbs: 5.5g; Protein: 29.8g; Fat: 13.6g

40. Prosciutto-Wrapped Scallops

- Serves: 4
- Prep Time: 3 min.
- Cook Time: 3 hr.

Ingredients

- 1 tbsp. extra-virgin olive oil
- lemon juice 1 tbsp.
- 12 large scallops, rinsed and patted dry
- Enough pepper & salt
- 1 ¼ oz. prosciutto, cut into 12 long strips

Directions:

1. Season the scallops with salt & pepper to taste before serving.
2. Wrap a prosciutto around the scallops. Set aside.
3. Add oil in crockpot and arrange on top the bacon-wrapped scallops.
4. Lemon juice, please.
5. Prepare on high for 3 hours or low for 1 hour.
6. Halfway during the Cook Time, turn the scallops.
7. Continue cooking until scallops are done.

Nutrition Info: KCal: 113; Carbs: 5g; Protein: 15.9g; Fat:8 g

Chapter 9: Dinner Recipes

41. Cheesy Ranch Chicken

- Serves: 6
- Prep Time: 5 min.
- Cook Time: 8 hr.

Ingredients

- chicken breasts, bones removed 1 ¼ pounds
- sugar-free ranch dressing ½ C.
- ½ C. cheddar cheese, shredded
- ½ C. parmesan cheese, shredded
- Cayenne pepper to taste

Directions:

1. Ranch dressing should be added to the slow cooker.
2. The chicken should be placed on top.
3. Add some hot pepper flakes for flavor.
4. Layer on the two cheeses.
5. Cook on low for 8 hours or high for 6 hours with the lid closed.

Nutrition Info: KCal: 267; Carbs: 7g; Protein: 25g; Fat: 15.1g

42. Classic Pork Adobo

- Serves: 6
- Cook Time: 12 hr.

Ingredients

- 2 pounds pork chops, sliced
- garlic, minced 4 cloves
- 1 onion, diced
- 2 bay leaves
- ¼ C. soy sauce
- ½ C. lemon juice, freshly squeezed
- 4 quail eggs, boiled and stripped

Directions:

1. Throw everything but the quail eggs into the slow cooker.
2. Mix it up thoroughly.
3. Put the lid on it, and cook it for 10 hours on high or 12 hours on low.
4. Quail eggs should be added 1 hour before the end of the Cook Time.

Nutrition Info: KCal: 371; Carbs: 6.4g; Protein: 40.7g; Fat: 24.1g

43. CrockPot Beef Picadillo

- Serves: 8
- Cook Time: 10 hr.

Ingredients

- crushed beef 2 pounds
- 20 green olives, pitted and diced
- 8 cloves of garlic, minced
- Enough pepper & salt
- chili powder 1 ½ tbsp.
- dried oregano 2 tbsp
- cinnamon powder 1 tsp.
- 1 C. tomatoes, diced
- 1 red onions, diced
- 2 Anaheim peppers, seeded and diced

Directions:

1. Throw everything into the slow cooker.
2. Mix it up thoroughly.
3. Cook covered for 8 hours on high heat or 10 hours on low.

Nutrition Info: KCal: 317; Carbs: 4.5g; Protein: 29.6g; Fat: 19.8g

44. Spicy Pork with Mapo Tofu

- Serves: 2
- Cook Time: 8 hr.

Ingredients

- 1 jalapeno, sliced
- 4 garlic cloves, sliced
- 1 tsp. Sichuan peppercorns
- 2 C. chicken broth
- 2 tbsp. vegetable oil
- 8 oz. crushed pork
- 1 ½-inch ginger, grated
- 1 tbsp. tomato paste
- 1-pound silken tofu, drained and cubed

Directions:

1. Render the crumbled pork in a skillet with oil heated over medium heat for three minutes while continually swirling.
2. Place everything except the silken tofu in the CrockPot with the meat.
3. Give a good stir.
4. Cook on high for 6 hours or low for 8 hours with the lid closed.
5. Add the tofu cubes an hour before the end of the Cook Time.

Nutrition Info: KCal:372; Carbs: 5.3g; Protein:30.3 g; Fat: 25.8g

45. Coconut Turmeric Chicken

- Serves: 8
- Cook Time: 8 hr.

Ingredients

- 2 inch-knob fresh ginger, grated
- 4 cloves of garlic, grated
- Enough pepper & salt
- 1 whole chicken, cut into pieces
- ½ C. coconut milk, unsweetened
- 2 inch-knob fresh turmeric, grated

Directions:

1. The Crock-Pot should be loaded with everything.
2. Cook, covered, for 6 hours on high heat or 8 hours on low.
3. Dice some onions and sprinkle on top.

Nutrition Info: KCal: 270; Carbs: 4.2g; Protein:24.5g; Fat: 18.9g; Sugar: 0g; Sodium: 883mg; Fiber: 1.6g

46. CrockPot Beef Rendang

- Serves: 8
- Cook Time: 10 hr.

Ingredients

- ½ C. desiccated coconut, toasted

- 1 tsp. salt
- 6 cloves of garlic, minced
- 1 C. coconut cream
- 1 beef shoulder, cut into chunks
- ½ C. cilantro leaves, diced
- ½ C. water
- 1 tbsp. coconut oil
- 6 dried birds eye chilies, diced
- 1 tsp. crushed cumin
- 2 tsp. crushed coriander
- 1 tsp. turmeric powder
- 6 kafir lime leaves
- 2 stalks lemon grass

Directions:

1. Put everything in the slow cooker except the cilantro leaves.
2. Mix it up thoroughly.
3. Cook covered for 8 hours on high heat or 10 hours on low.
4. Sprinkle cilantro on top after cooking.

Nutrition Info: KCal:305; Carbs: 6.5g; Protein: 32.3g; Fat: 18.7g

47. Citrus infused Chicken Breasts

- Serves 2-4

Ingredients

- 1 tbsp. of lemon pepper seasoning

- Salt and pepper
- Cooking spray
- Water
- 1 can cream of chicken soup
- Juice of half a lemon
- 2 large oranges, 1 juiced, 1 sliced
- 4 boneless and skinless chicken breasts

Directions

1. Spray some cooking spray on the bottom of the slow cooker.
2. Salt and pepper the chicken breasts.
3. Arrange the orange slices in the slow cooker's bottom. Place the oranges on top of the chicken breasts.
4. Add some lemon and orange juice and lemon pepper to the soup before serving.
5. Put in half a can of water and stir. We recommend using a whisk to ensure a smooth finish.
6. Add it to the slow cooker with the chicken.
7. Preparation time is 3 hours on HIGH or 6 hours on LOW.
8. Accompany with rice and the greens of your choice.

Nutrition Info: KCal 670, Fat 37.07 g, Carbs 34.52 g, Protein 45.31 g

48. Homey Tomato Soup

- Serves 4

Ingredients

- 1 red pepper, diced
- 1 tsp. oregano
- 1 tsp. basil
- 28 oz. diced tomatoes, canned, drained and rinsed
- 4 C. vegetable stock
- ½ C. cashews, soaked
- ½ C. sundried tomatoes
- 4 cloves garlic, minced
- ½ tsp. red pepper flakes
- Salt and pepper
- 8 oz. tomato paste

Optional

- Vegan Parmesan
- Fresh basil

Directions

1. To speed up the cooking process, soak the cashews in water.
2. Put everything into the slow cooker except the cashews. Cover and simmer for 6 hours on low heat.
3. Immersion blender the cashews that have been soaking.
4. Serve warm with desired toppings.

Nutrition Info: KCal 284, Fat 9 g, Carbs 42 g, Protein 10 g

49. *Butternut Squash Soup*

- Serves 2 (refrigerate leftovers)

Ingredients

- 5 C. butternut squash, cubed
- Enough pepper & salt
- ¼ C. heavy cream, optional
- 1 pinch freshly crushed nutmeg
- Water, about 3 C. or veggie stock
- 2 cloves garlic
- 1 small onion, diced

Directions

1. Put the squash, garlic, and onion into the slow cooker. Put enough water or vegetable stock on top to cover. Put in as much salt and pepper as you like. Add the nutmeg and give it a good stir.
2. Time it for 3–4 hours on LOW or 1–2 hours on HIGH.
3. When the squash is tender enough to mash, turn to an immersion blender to smooth up the soup.
4. Heavy cream, if used, should be added during the final 30 minutes of simmering for a creamier soup. Merge the ingredients together by stirring.
5. Try it out and season it with salt, pepper, and nutmeg if you think it needs it.
6. Prepare and serve quickly.

Nutrition Info: (with vegie stock – no cream)

KCal 187, Fat 0.2 g, Carbs 43 g, Protein 10 g

50. Spicy Indian Beef Roast

- Serves: 8
- Cook Time: 10 hr.

Ingredients

- 2 red onions, diced
- 2 tbsp. lemon juice, freshly squeezed
- 4 cloves of garlic, minced
- 1 ½-inch ginger, minced
- 25 curry leaves
- 1 serrano pepper, minced
- 1 tbsp. meat masala
- 2 tbsp. coconut oil
- 1 tsp. black mustard seed
- 2 ½ pounds grass-fed beef roast

Directions:

1. The Crock-Pot should be loaded with everything.
2. Stir it up really well.
3. Lock the lid in place and cook for 6 hours on high or 10 hours on low.

Nutrition Info: KCal: 222; Carbs: 1.1g; Protein: 31.3g; Fat:10.4 g

51. Popeye's Turkey Soup

- Serves 8

Ingredients

- 2 C. low-sodium chicken stock
- 1 tsp. black pepper
- Extra virgin olive oil
- 1 tsp. rosemary

- 1 turkey breast (2.5 pounds)
- 6 C. spinach, diced
- 1 medium onion, diced.
- 4 garlic cloves, grated
- ½ tsp. thyme
- 1 tsp. salt

Directions

1. Brush slow cooker with extra virgin olive oil and set slow cooker to medium.
2. Slice turkey breast into ½" cubes.
3. To brown turkey breast, heat 4 tablespoons of extra virgin olive oil in a skillet.
4. Cover and simmer on low for 8 hours with turkey breast, spinach, onion, garlic, chicken stock, rosemary, thyme, salt, and pepper.
5. Leave it to simmer for 4 hours.

Nutrition Info: KCal 193, Fat 6 g, Carbs 8.8 g, Protein 25 g

52. *Italian Meatball Soup*

- Serves 8

Ingredients

- 1 (10-oz.) bag frozen soup vegetables
- Some fresh oregano (optional)
- 2 (14½-oz.) cans Italian-style tomatoes, diced, undrained
- 2 (12-oz.) bags Italian-style turkey meatballs, thawed and cooked

- 1 (15-oz.) can black beans, rinsed, drained
- 1 (14-oz.) can seasoned chicken broth with roasted garlic

Directions

1. Mix everything except the oregano in a bowl.
2. Put the ingredients in a slow cooker and simmer them for 6 to 7 hours on the LOW setting.
3. If you're in a rush, you can also cook it on HIGH for 3 to 3 12 hours.
4. Place in a bowl and, if using, season with oregano.
5. Prepare and savor.

Nutrition Info: KCal 287, Fat 13 g, Carbs 30 g, Protein 16 g

53. CrockPot Gingered Pork Stew

- Serves: 9
- Cook Time: 12 hr.

Ingredients

- crushed cinnamon 2 tbsp.
- crushed ginger 2 tbsp.
- 3 pounds pork shoulder, cut into cubes
- 2 C. homemade chicken broth
- Enough pepper & salt
- 1 tbsp. crushed allspice
- crushed cloves 1 ½ tsp.
- crushed nutmeg 1 tbsp.
- 1 tbsp. paprika

Directions:

1. Throw everything into the slow cooker.
2. Mix it up thoroughly.
3. Put the lid on it, and cook it for 10 hours on high or 12 hours on low.

Nutrition Info: KCal: 425; Carbs: 4.2g; Protein: 38.7g; Fat: 27.4g

54. Three-Bean Vegan Chili

- Serves 4

Ingredients

- ½ (15.5-oz.) can kidney beans
- ½ (15.5-oz.) can chickpeas
- Fresh cilantro leaves (optional)
- 2 tbsp. vegetable oil
- ½ (28-oz.) can diced tomatoes
- 1 tbsp. chili powder
- 1 tsp. crushed cumin
- 1 tsp. dried oregano
- 2 tbsp. tomato paste
- 1 ¾ C. water
- ½ (15.5-oz.) can black beans
- 1 onion, finely diced
- 1 red bell pepper, finely diced
- 1 green bell pepper, finely diced
- 1 jalapeño pepper, seeded and minced
- 2 cloves garlic, minced

- ¼ tsp. salt

Directions

1. Spread the oil across the inside of a 6-quart slow cooker. Toss in the chopped onion, bell peppers, jalapeo, minced garlic, and a pinch of salt. Put in the tomato paste, tomato sauce, diced tomatoes, chili powder, cumin, oregano, and water.
2. Cook, covered, on LOW heat for 4 hours.
3. The beans should be drained and rinsed before being added to the slow cooker and mixed together. Add another 2–4 hours of cooking time while covered.
4. Top each serving with cilantro.

Nutrition Info: KCal 245, Fat 2.9 g, Carbs 45.1 g, Protein 12.9 g

55. Beef Tomato Lentil Soup

- Serves 6-8

Ingredients

- 10 cherry tomatoes, to garnish
- Enough pepper & salt
- 2 pounds crushed beef
- ¼ C. prepared yellow mustard
- ¼ C. sour cream, to garnish
- ½ C. green bell pepper, diced
- ½ C. red bell pepper, diced
- 6 C. beef stock

- 2 C. dry green lentils
- ½ C. creamed corn
- 1 (28-oz.) can diced tomatoes

Directions

1. The ground beef should be browned in a frying skillet and the fat drained. Put the lentils, corn, tinned tomatoes, mustard, green bell pepper, and red bell pepper into the slow cooker along with the stock.
2. Prepare on high for 1 hour and 15 minutes or on low for 3 hours and 15 minutes. Cherry tomatoes and sour cream make a lovely garnish.

Nutrition Info: KCal 299, Fat 11 g, Carbs 29 g, Protein 26.6 g

56. Silky Broccoli and Cheese Soup

- Serves 8

Ingredients

- 1 tsp. black pepper
- Extra virgin olive oil
- 4 tbsp. ghee
- 3 C. broccoli florets
- cashews, soaked overnight, diced ½ C.
- cheddar, grated ½ C.
- 2 C. low-sodium chicken stock
- 1 C. coconut cream
- 1 tsp. coconut flour

- salt 1 tsp.

Directions

1. Heat ghee in skillet over medium heat.
2. Mix coconut flour into skillet quickly.
3. Add coconut cream, mix until smooth, and set aside.
4. Brush slow cooker with extra virgin olive oil, and set on high.
5. Place broccoli in slow cooker with chicken stock, salt, black pepper, cashews. Blend together and let sit covered for 10 minutes.
6. Cook, combining the coconut cream mixture with the cheese, for 3 hours.

Nutrition Info: KCal 216, Fat 20 g, Carbs 7 g, Protein 5 g

57. Split Pea Soup

- Serves 4

Ingredients

- 1 pound split peas, rinsed and dried
- 6 C. vegetable broth
- 1 onion, diced
- 1 bay leaf
- 1 tsp. thyme
- Salt and pepper (to taste)
- 1 tsp. cumin
- 1 tsp. sage
- 2 carrots, stripped and diced

- 2 celery stalks, diced
- 3 cloves garlic, minced

Directions

1. Put everything in the crock pot and set it to low. Slowly heat for at least 4 hours with the lid on.
2. Serve as is, or blend until smooth with an immersion blender.

Nutrition Info: KCal 272, Fat 1 g, Carbs 75 g, Protein 25 g

58. *Chipotle Chicken Soup*

- Serves 4

Ingredients

- 1 tsp. black pepper
- 1 tsp. cumin
- 1 tsp. salt
- 1 C. onion, sliced
- ¼ C. chipotle chili in adobo sauce, diced
- 4 C. chicken stock
- ½ tsp. coriander
- 1 C. poblano pepper, sliced
- 1 avocado, sliced
- 1 C. Monterey Jack cheese, shredded
- ½ C. fresh cilantro
- 1 pound boneless chicken pieces
- 1 tbsp. olive oil

Directions

1. The chicken should be cut into small pieces.
2. Season the chicken with salt, pepper, cumin, and coriander and drizzle it with olive oil.
3. Add the chicken, poblano, onion, chipotle, and adobo sauce to a slow cooker and simmer on low for 8 hours.
4. Toss in the chicken stock, cover, and simmer on high for four hours, checking occasionally to make sure the chicken is done.
5. Avocado slices, Monterey Jack cheese, and chopped cilantro provide a delicious topping for the soup.

Nutrition Info: KCal 363, Fat 20.9 g, Carbs 10.5 g, Protein 33.7 g

59. *French Canadian Pea Soup*

- Serves 8-10

Ingredients

- 2 C. yellow peas
- 1 ham hock or 6 oz. salted pork belly
- 1 onion, finely diced
- ½ tsp. dried savory (optional)
- Salt and black pepper, to taste
- 6 C. water

Directions

1. Soak the peas in water overnight. Rinse and sort the peas if needed. Drain.
2. Add peas, onion, savory, if using, and ham hock or salted pork belly to the slow cooker.
3. Cook, covered, on LOW for 8 to 10 hours.
4. Take out the salt pork or ham hock. Remove any remaining meat off the bone or salted pork once it has cooled for a few minutes.
5. Put the meat back in the slow cooker, toss it around so it cooks evenly, and set the timer for another 10 to 15 minutes.
6. Add salt and pepper to taste if necessary.
7. Use crusty bread and serve hot.

Nutrition Info: KCal 191, Fat 6 g, Carbs 24 g, Protein 10 g

60. Cajun Sausage and White Bean Soup

- Serves 6

Ingredients

- 1 tbsp. red wine vinegar
- Salt and pepper
- 8 C. chicken broth, low-sodium
- 2 stalks celery, diced
- 4 sprigs fresh thyme
- 8 C. collard greens, leaves only, cut to 1-inch pieces
- 1 pound dried Great Northern beans
- ½ pound Cajun andouille sausage, sliced
- 1 large onion, diced

Directions

1. Put the remaining three ingredients aside.
2. Cooked beans, sausage, onion, celery, thyme, and chicken broth should be combined in a slow cooker.
3. Cook covered for 7–8 hours on LOW or 4–5 hours on HIGH. Tender beans are ideal.
4. Take off the stems of the thyme and add the collard greens. Greens should be cooked for an additional 15 minutes with the lid on.
5. Combine the vinegar with the salt and pepper.

Nutrition Info: KCal 393, Fat 8 g, Carbs 51 g, Protein 30 g

Chapter 10: Dessert Recipes

61. Mandarin Cream

- Servings: 2
- Cook Time: 2 Hr.

Ingredients:

- 1 tbsp. ginger, grated
- 3 tbsp. sugar
- 3 mandarins, stripped and diced
- 2 tbsp. agave nectar
- ½ C. coconut cream

Directions:

1. Add the ginger, sugar, mandarins, and the rest of the ingredients to the crock pot and stir to combine. Cover and simmer on High for 2 hours.
2. Use an immersion blender to smooth the cream, then serve it in individual dishes in the fridge.

Nutrition Info: KCal100, fat 4, fiber 5, carbs 6, protein 7

62. Mascarpone With Strawberry Jelly

- Servings:6
- Cook Time: 1 Hr.

Ingredients:

- 2 C. strawberries, diced
- 1 tbsp. gelatin
- 3 tbsp. sugar
- ¼ C. of water
- 1 C. mascarpone

Directions:

1. Mix strawberries with sugar and blend the mixture until smooth.
2. Transfer it in the Crock Pot and cook on High for 1 hr..
3. Meanwhile, mix water with gelatin.
4. Whisk the mascarpone well.
5. When the strawberry mixture is cooked, cool it little and add gelatin. Carefully mix it.
6. Pour the strawberry mixture in the ramekins and refrigerate for 2 hr..

7. Then top the jelly with whisked mascarpone.

Nutrition Info: 125 kCal, 9g protein, 11g Carbs, 5.5g fat

63. Easy Monkey Rolls

- Servings: 8
- Cook Time: 3 Hr.

Ingredients:

- 1 tbsp. liquid honey
- 1 tbsp. sugar
- 2 eggs, beaten
- 1-pound cinnamon rolls, dough
- 2 tbsp. butter, melted

Directions:

1. Divide the dough for the cinnamon rolls into 8 pieces.
2. The rolls should be placed inside a Crock Pot that has been lined with baking paper.
3. Cream together the butter and sugar until it forms a ball. Toss the ingredients together with a whisk.
4. Spread the cinnamon roll dough out evenly and pour the egg mixture on top.
5. Cover and cook for 3 hours on High heat.

Nutrition Info: 266 kCal, 4.9g protein, 32.6g Carbs, 13.3g fat,

64. Lemony Orange Marmalade

- Servings: 8
- Cook Time: 3 Hrs.

Ingredients:

- Juice of 2 lemons
- 3 lbs. sugar
- 1 lb. oranges, stripped and cut into segments
- 1-pint water

Directions:

1. Mix oranges, sugar, water, and lemon juice in the Crock Pot insert.
2. Cover the slow cooker and set the timer to High for three hours.
3. Cold is best when served.

Nutrition Info: KCal: 100, Total Fat: 4g, Fiber: 4g, Total Carbs: 12g, Protein: 4g

65. Braised Pears

- Servings: 6
- Cook Time: 2.5 Hr.

Ingredients:

- 6 pears
- 2 C. wine
- 1 tbsp. sugar

- 1 cinnamon stick

Directions:

1. Put the halved pears in the slow cooker.
2. Put the top back on and add the rest of the ingredients.
3. For around 2.5 hours on High, prepare the pears.
4. Serve the pears with hot wine mixture.

Nutrition Info: 210 kCal, 1.1g protein, 38g Carbs, 1.1g fat

66. Stuffed Peaches

- Servings:4
- Cook Time: 20 Min.

Ingredients:

- 4 peaches, halved, pitted
- 4 pecans
- 1 tbsp. maple syrup
- 2 oz goat cheese, crumbled

Directions:

1. Fill every peach half with pecan and sprinkle with maple syrup.
2. The next step is to spread the goat cheese over the top of the fruit in the Crock Pot.
3. Cook the peaches for 20 minutes with the lid closed, over High heat.

Nutrition Info: 234 kCal, 7.2g protein, 19.7g Carbs, 15.5g fat

67. Cinnamon Rice Milk Cocktail

- Servings: 6
- Cook Time: 1.5 Hr.

Ingredients:

- 1 C. long-grain rice
- ½ C. agave syrup
- 3 C. of water
- 1 tsp. crushed cinnamon
- 1 banana, diced

Directions:

1. The rice should be placed in the processor.
2. Put the mixture in a blender and add water to thin it up.
3. Next, strain the liquid and add it to the slow cooker.
4. Blend in some agave nectar and ground cinnamon. The liquid should be cooked for 1.5 hours on High.
5. The next step is to pour the boiling liquid into the blender or food processor.
6. Blend in a banana until it's completely smooth.

Nutrition Info: 215 kCal, 2.4g protein, 51.5g Carbs, 0.3g fat

68. Mango Cream Dessert

- Servings: 4
- Cook Time: 1 Hr.

Ingredients:

- 1 mango, sliced
- 14 oz. coconut cream

Directions:

1. Add mango and cream to the insert of Crock Pot.
2. Put the cooker's lid on and set the Cook Time to 1 hr. on High settings.
3. Serve.

Nutrition Info: KCal: 150, Total Fat: 12g, Fiber: 2g, Total Carbs: 6g, Protein: 1g

69. Apricot Spoon Cake

- Servings: 10
- Cook Time: 2.5 Hr.

Ingredients:

- 2 C. cake mix
- 1 C. milk
- 1 C. apricots, canned, pitted, diced, with juice
- 2 eggs, beaten
- 1 tbsp. sunflower oil

Directions:

1. Mix milk with cake mix and egg.
2. Then sunflower oil and blend the mixture until smooth.
3. The Crock Pot should then be lined with baking paper.

4. Put the cake mix batter in the slow cooker and gently press down before covering it.
5. Bake the cake for 2.5 hours on High.
6. Then transfer the cooked cake in the plate and top with apricots and apricot juice.
7. Leave the cake until it is warm and cut into servings.

Nutrition Info: 268 kCal, 4.5g protein, 43.8g Carbs, 8.6g fat

70. Baked Goat Cheese Balls

- Servings:6
- Cook Time: 1 Hr.

Ingredients:

- 1 tsp. butter
- 1 tbsp. breadcrumbs
- 8 oz goat cheese
- 4 tbsp. sesame seeds
- 1 tsp. of sugar powder

Directions:

1. Mix goat cheese with sugar powder and breadcrumbs.
2. Make the medium size balls and coat them in the sesame seeds.
3. Melt the butter and pour it in the Crock Pot.
4. Place the balls in a single layer in the slow cooker and cover.
5. Prepare the sweet for 1 hour on high heat.

Nutrition Info: 217 kCal, 12.8g protein, 3.5g Carbs, 17.1g fat

Conclusion

When one investigates the world of culinary arts in greater depth, they will frequently come face to face with a convoluted network of techniques, varieties of food, and different kinds of implements. The "The Complete Crock Pot Cookbook: 2000 Days of Flavorful and Tasty Recipes | Expert Tips for Newbies to Create Slow-Cooked Culinary Wonders Without Breaking the Bank" is our guide to the rediscovered joy of using a crock pot. Our journey is an immersion into the rediscovered joy of cooking with a crock pot. The fact that a piece of kitchenware that was once considered antiquated is now held in high esteem as a legend of the contemporary kitchen is evidence that every urban legend will, in due time, make a comeback.

The primary focus of our inquiry is the rediscovery of the crock pot not only as a tool for cooking but also as a collaborator in the kitchen. Many other methods of cooking yield tastes that are simpler and less nuanced than those produced by this method's particular slow-cooking strategy, which permits the components to blend over a longer period of time. Regarding this matter, it is vitally important not to underestimate the transformative capacity of the crock pot. The meals in our carefully curated assortment cover a broad spectrum, from savory broths to decadent desserts and everything in between, ensuring that there is an option that will appeal to each and every one of our readers. Each recipe is meant to serve as an illustration of the resourcefulness and versatility that is possessed by this ever-relevant kitchen tool.

This cookbook was created with the intention of achieving the highest possible level of convenience in order to meet the requirements of those living in today's fast-paced culture, in which time can frequently appear to be a scarce commodity. Even the busiest of people are able to create exquisite delights without being bound to the kitchen because the recipes only demand a short amount of time to put together before they are left to their own devices. This allows even the busiest of people to take use of the recipes. An range of tasty dishes that can be prepared with a minimum of effort, spanning the gap between gourmet and everyday fare, is the expression of our promise to you.

The book featured a lot more than just recipes; in addition to discussing the culture, history, and development of the slow cooker, the book also included several recipes. In this tutorial, we covered a wide variety of topics, such as the science behind slow cooking, how to get the most out of your equipment, and how to choose the finest slow cooker for your specific needs and preferences. Not only will the readers be able to follow recipes, but they will also be able to design and create new dishes while still being aware of the core components that make up each meal.

This cookbook exceeds its function as merely a guide by blending together aspects from the past and the present, as well as aspects that are traditional and those that are contemporary. It encapsulates the ethos of a culture that values the tried-and-true in roughly the same proportion as it does the novel. Because it is a location where memories from the kitchens of our ancestors come together with the inventions of the current day, the crock pot, as a result, is symbolic of our connection with food. It is a place where the past and the present collide.

Although it has been a pleasure to guide you through this exciting culinary journey, the conclusion of this book marks the beginning of your very own journey, and I cannot wait to see where it takes you! What should one ultimately take away from this? The crock pot is more than just a piece of kitchenware; it is also a symbol for resilience, advancement, and an unquenchable desire for tasty cuisine. And if there's one concept that I really wish would resonate with you, it would be this one: Patience is more than simply a virtue when it comes to the realm of cooking; it's a flavor in and of itself. Embrace the slow, savor the journey, and use your crock pot to serve as a continual reminder that with sufficient time, even the most basic components can be transformed into works of art.

Made in the USA
Columbia, SC
24 October 2024